REVISED AND UPDATED

Art In History

Ancient Greek Art

Susie Hodge

Heinemann Library
Chicago, Illinois

Customer Service 888-454-2279
Visit our website at www.heinemannraintree.com

Design by Victoria Bevan, Michelle Lisseter, and Q2A Media
Illustrations by Oxford Illustrators
Printed and bound in Hong Kong by WKT

10 09 08 07 06
10 9 8 7 6 5 4 3 2 1

New edition ISBNs: 1 40348 766 9 (hardback)
                          1 40348 774 X (paperback)

The Library of Congress has cataloged the first edition as follows:
Hodge, Susie, 1960–
    Ancient Greek art / Susie Hodge.
        p. cm. -- (Art in history)
    Includes bibliographical references and index.
    Summary: Examines the art of ancient Greece, including mosaics,
pottery, sculpture, architecture, and paintings.
        ISBN 1-57572-551-7 (lib. bdg.)
        1. Art. Greek--Juvenile literature. 2. Art, Ancient--Greece--
Juvenile literature. [1. Art, Greek. 2. Art, Ancient.]
i. Title. II. Series: Hodge, Susie, 1960– Art in history.
N5630.H63   1997
709'.38--dc21   97–20674
                                                    CIP
                                                     AC

Acknowledgments
The publishers would like to thank the following for permission to reproduce photographs:
AKG photo p. **10**, Metropolitan Museum of Art, N.Y. p. **14**; Ancient Art & Architecture Collection p. **18**, R. Sheridan pp. **8**, **9**, **12**, **15**, **19** (both), **28**; Bridgeman Art Library, British Museum pp. **13**, **21**, House of Masks, Delos, Greece p. **16**, K & B News Foto p. **29**, Museo & Gallerie Nazionali di Capodimonte, Naples p. **17**, National Archaeological Museum, Athens p. **20**, Vatican Museums & Galleries p. **5**; British Museum, London p. **23**; Corbis, W. Kaehler p. **4**, M. Nicholson p. **27**, G. D. Orti p. **6**; C. M. Dixon pp. **11**, **25**; B. O. Giraudon p. **26**; Michael Holford p. **24**; Werner Forman Archive, British Museum p. **22**, Private Collection New York p. **7**.

Cover picture of Priestess of Dionysus, 4th century BC, reproduced with permission of The Art Archive/Archeological Museum Paestum / Dagli Orti.

Every effort has been made to contact copyright holders of any material reproduced in this book. Any omissions will be rectified in subsequent printings if notice is given to the publishers.

The paper used to print this book comes from sustainable resources.

CONTENTS

Some words are shown in bold, **like this**.
You can find out what they mean by looking in the glossary.

WHO WERE THE ANCIENT GREEKS?

The earliest evidence we have of Greek culture is on the island of Crete. From about 3000 BC to 1380 BC, the Minoan people on the island of Crete farmed, built palaces and towns, and developed their own artistic style.

From about 2000 BC, the Mycenaeans on the Greek mainland developed their own civilization. They traded with and fought against the Minoans and were influenced by Minoan art.

City states

Ancient Greece was made up of islands and two separate pieces of mainland that were covered with mountains.

Dolphin **Fresco**, Knossos in Crete, c. 1580 BC, fresco

The walls of Minoan palaces were richly decorated. These leaping dolphins are from the Queen's Room in the palace of the legendary King Minos.

Four periods

After the Mycenaeans, Greek art is usually divided into four main periods:
Geometric (1100–700 BC), **Archaic** (700–500 BC), **Classical** (500–323 BC), and **Hellenistic** (323–100 BC).
The most famous is the Classical period. It was the period when Greek art was at its best.

It was difficult to travel and hard to think of these places as being part of the same country. Early Greeks did not consider themselves Greek at all.

Greek civilization developed as many city states. Each was based on a city that controlled the farmland and villages around it. City states had different laws and ways of doing things. But they were united by one language. Different city states were powerful at different times. Sometimes they fought each other and sometimes they joined forces. They were all united against the Persian invasion in 490 BC. But after they had defeated the Persians, they fought each other again.

Alexander the Great

From 336 BC onward, Alexander the Great united the city states so they could conquer the Persian Empire. But when he died, Greece split up again. Weakened by this split, Greece was gradually conquered by the Romans.

Achilles and Ajax Playing Checkers, Exekias, c. 540 BC, 24 inches (58 cm), **black-figure style** *vase*

Greek pottery was beautifully made. Even if they were made to hold wine or oil, pots were called vases. Artists painted stories on them. This is a story from a Greek myth. The faces are painted in profile, but the eyes are seen from the front.

MATERIALS AND METHODS

Mycenaean artists usually worked for the king. They trained as **apprentices** from a young age and worked together in workshops. Much of their work was traded for goods from other countries.

Later, art and craft skills were passed down through the family. A boy learned skills by helping his father and his father's workmen and slaves. Few women were artists. Each workshop specialized in a particular kind of art or craft, such as stone carving or wall painting. Usually fewer than ten men worked in one workshop.

How artists were treated

At first, artists were seen as unimportant, common workmen because their hands got dirty when they worked. But by about 480 BC, art had become important. **Architects**, painters, and sculptors were seen as skilled craftsmen, worthy of respect.

By the 5th century BC, the city states (such as Athens) were settled enough to devote time to art. Artists developed their skills to produce more lifelike work.

Myron worked in the early Classical period. He liked to show movement frozen in time. This athlete is caught just as he is about to throw the discus. Sports were important in many Greek city states and are often shown in statues and on painted vases.

Discus Thrower, *Myron*, c. 450 BC, 4 feet (1.25 m), originally bronze

Spiral ring, c. 5th century BC, gold

Craftspeople used many different materials for jewelry and artwork. This spiral ring was expertly crafted in gold and would have been worn by a wealthy person.

Artists' equipment

Greek artists painted on walls, wood or **marble** panels, **terracotta** slabs, and sometimes pieces of ivory, leather, **parchment**, papyrus, or linen. Wood was the most common choice. It was given a white undercoat first. Brushes and pens were made from reeds (tall grasses). Painters used **tempera** and fresco on walls. They used tempera and **encaustic** on wood or marble.

The usual materials for sculpture were marble and **bronze**. Sculptors occasionally used **limestone**, terracotta, and wood, and sometimes gold and ivory with a wooden center. They used solid gold and silver for very special sculptures.

SIGNS AND SYMBOLS

The first Greek alphabet was made about 700 BC, at the start of the Archaic period. The Greeks developed it from earlier Phoenician writing, which used symbols to represent sounds. Phoenician writing was read from right to left.

Two hundred years later, the Greeks changed it to read from left to right, as we do today. They added new symbols to form an alphabet of 24 letters. (The word *alphabet* comes from the first two letters, α, or alpha, and β, or beta.) A written language meant that the Greeks could pass on ideas and information more easily.

Geometric period

After about 1100 BC, Greek artists replaced the flowing Mycenaean patterns with lines and angles. People were shown as symbols (circles, rectangles, and triangles). They were not shown as realistic images.

Written in stone

Much of what we know about the ancient Greeks comes from reading the inscriptions (writings) that they carved in stone.

This huge amphora (tall vase with two handles) was used for storing wine or oil. The geometric patterns show simplified people and "key" shapes. The patterns resemble the writing that the Greeks developed (see opposite page, top right).

Geometric style vase, c. 700 BC, height 5 feet (1.55 m)

α β χ δ ε φ γ η ι φ κ λ μ

How symbols developed

Ancient Greek artists drew a spear as the symbol of lightning (or a thunderbolt) coming from thunderclouds to earth. They developed many more symbols, like the owl that became a symbol of Athena, and later Athens. Athenian coins were made with owls on one side. Today, we use many of the ancient Greeks' symbols in horoscopes.

ν ο π θ ρ σ τ υ ϖ ω ξ ψ ζ

As time passed, more writing was done on parchment or other paper-like substances on which a pen and ink could be used. This was much quicker than carving.

The writings of Greek historians, philosophers, poets, and playwrights have taught us a lot about how people lived and what they thought.

*Departure of Triptolemos, Makron, c. 480 BC, height 8¼ inches (21 cm), **red-figure style** vase*

The Greeks told stories in pictures, too. This vase, from the beginning of the Classical period, shows the god Triptolemos holding stalks of corn and a dish while sitting on a wheeled throne with wings. Persephone stands in front of him with a torch and a jug. Two other goddesses stand behind them. Triptolemos is about to take the corn to earth to teach humans how to grow crops.

MISSING PICTURES

Why are there so many ancient Greek pots and statues? Why are there so few paintings? How do we know that paintings existed? Well, we know that the Greeks produced beautiful paintings, particularly during the Archaic, Classical, and Hellenistic periods, for these reasons:

- Ancient writers described them.
- Some fragments have survived.
- The Romans copied them later on.
- Vases that survived show the skills of painters.

The dry climate of the desert preserved many Egyptian paintings, but the Greek climate can be damp. Damp air destroys paintings and decays wood. Many Greek paintings were also destroyed when fighting between city states led to fires in the cities.

Head of a Woman, 1300 BC, fresco

This fragment of a painting comes from a **frieze** that was inside a Greek palace. The woman's dress and the style of the painting come from Minoan times, but her face is Mycenaean. She is painted in profile, with her eye shown from the front. The paint has faded, but you can see how flat, yet decorative, early paintings were. Composition, or layout, was more important than being realistic.

Sacrifice with Musicians, Corinth in Greece, c. 520–500 BC, tempera on wood panel

This painting still makes the people look flat and shows them from the side, but now artists were beginning to paint folds in clothes and to put one person behind another to show three-dimensional space. In this painting, as in ancient Egyptian art, boys and men are painted with darker skin than girls and women.

Color and decoration

Paintings were often used to decorate buildings. At first all paintings looked flat. The artists did not try to make anything look rounded or real. This is true of Minoan and Mycenaean art. But by studying real people, some Greek artists discovered how to make figures look lifelike. By the 5th century BC, artists still used bright colors, but with light and shade. This gave a three-dimensional effect. They also created atmosphere and mood.

Paint palette

Paint colors were limited to what could be produced naturally. Brown, reds, and yellow came from earth, rocks, and clay; white came from chalk; black came from soot; blue came from a kind of glass; green came from copper; and purple came from a special seashell. **Pigments** were mixed with egg white to make a paste for painting.

POTTERY PICTURES

Decorating a pot is different from painting a picture on a flat surface. Some parts of a pot curve away from the viewer. The pot shape makes an oddly shaped frame. So, Greek artists skillfully adjusted their designs to fit.

Birth of Athena, c. 400 BC, red-figure style vase

In Greek legend, the god Hephaistos made a special ax. When it was time for Athena to be born, Hephaistos used the ax to cut Zeus's head open; Athena came out of his head. Even when the pictures of that story become distorted on this vase shape, they are clearly balanced and decorative.

Vase shapes

Greek pots were so well made that thousands of pieces have survived. They were strong and practical, but also skillfully painted. Different shaped vases had different uses. For example, amphorae were used for storing wine. Kraters were for holding wine and water.

Black-figure style

Artists painted patterns and pictures on red-clay pots with a mixture of clay, water, and wood ash. They scratched details into the clay with a pointed tool and left the background red. They began firing the pot in a kiln (a special hot oven to bake clay). Then, they closed all the openings in the kiln. The lack of air made the pot turn black. When air was let in again, the painted parts stayed black and the rest of the pot turned red.

Red-figure style

In about 510 BC, this black-figure style was taken over by the red-figure style. The method was the same, but this time the background was black and the figures appeared red. Artists outlined details in black, using a fine brush. Curves are easier to draw with a brush than a scratching tool, so red-figure vases are more expressive.

Make a Greek tile

Materials:

- **Self-hardening clay**
- **Water**
- **Carving and cutting tools**
- **Brushes**
- **Paints**
- **Glue**

1. Warm some clay in your hands. Shape it into a tile by rolling, pressing, and cutting.

2. Smooth the clay with a little water and carve a picture using a stick. Leave it to dry.

3. Mix poster paint with some glue and paint your tile brightly.

This large amphora was made for a special procession that went to the **Parthenon** every four years to make an offering to the goddess Athena. Because the horses are rearing and the man is leaning forward in the chariot, the picture appears to be moving as it curves around the vase.

Wine vase, Athens in Greece, c. 500 BC, black-figure style vase, ceramic

THE BREAK WITH TRADITION

Ancient Greek art developed over centuries, from the Minoans in 3000 BC onward. It also borrowed artistic ideas from other people with whom it came into contact through trade.

At first, art was mainly about the afterlife. Painted tombs, statues, and masks were made to help the dead travel to the next world. This was similar to the Egyptian traditions. Egyptians were one of the peoples with whom the Greeks traded.

Egyptian rules

Many artists working in the Geometric period followed Egyptian rules. They did not paint or carve what they saw. Rather, they just showed what they knew to be there. For example, images of people made from simple shapes were recognizable but not realistic.

Wedding Procession, by Exekias, Athens in Greece, c. 540 BC, height 1 foot, 6 inches (47 cm), black-figure style vase, ceramic

Exekias was one of the finest black-figure painters of Athens. This amphora includes some white and red paint to show details, although the picture follows ancient rules of making the humans and animals look as simple as possible. Soon, the rules were forgotten, as it became important to make everything look lifelike.

Archaic art

During the Archaic period, artists began producing temples and huge statues. The statues were again made according to ancient Egyptian rules. They look stiff and awkward. But on pots, more flowing red-figure painting took over from black-figure painting.

The golden age

Early in 500 BC, many artists, especially those in more settled city states like Athens, began to produce more lifelike art. They tried to make flat pictures look three-dimensional and make stiff sculptures look natural. They became fascinated with **proportion** and **symmetry**.

Art thrived when city states were not at war with each other. Painters began using shadows and highlights. They also studied perspective (how to make things look far away) and foreshortening (how to make things look close). They invented **optical illusion** by making flat pictures look real. They also painted objects from different angles.

Changing art

By the Hellenistic period, art was less connected with religion. Artists became more interested in the problems of creating beautiful images. Writers took more of an interest in art. Art had changed a lot.

Tombstone of Hegeso, c. 420 BC, stone

This carved picture is called a relief. Hegeso sits, selecting jewelry from her servant. See how realistic the women and their draped clothes look.

MARVELOUS MOSAICS

The Greeks developed many ways of making pictures. They made frescoes, **murals**, **reliefs**, encaustic, and mosaics.

Mosaics are patterns made with hundreds of tiny squares of colored glass, pebbles, gold, or marble. Ancient Greek artists invented mosaic pictures. At first they only made them on floors, but artists later made wall mosaics as well.

How mosaics were made
Artists collected stones, glass, or gold and cut them into square or diamond shapes. These were called tessellated mosaics. They used glass sparingly on floors, but generously on walls. The mosaics were sorted into groups of colors. Artists spread a type of cement mixture on the floor or wall. They followed a previously drawn plan that showed them where to put the colors. They pushed in the mosaics while the cement was still wet. By 300 BC artists were so good at mosaics they could cut tiny pieces of brilliant colors and produce very detailed pictures.

Dionysus Riding a Leopard, from the House of Masks, Delos in Greece, c. AD 180, mosaic

Mosaics are often colorful, detailed, and shiny. Because the cement was strong, many ancient Greek mosaics have remained clear. Like most other Greek art of the time, the subject of this picture is animals, monsters, and myths, with measured patterns around them.

The Alexander Mosaic, *from Naples in Italy, 1st century* BC, *11 feet, 3 inches (3.42 m), mosaic (from a copy of a work by Philoxenos, c. 300* BC)

Alexander the Great conquered a huge empire, stretching from Egypt to India. This famous but damaged wall mosaic shows his victory over the Persians. It is a Roman copy of a Greek painting made during the late 4th century BC. The Romans borrowed the use of mosaics from the Greeks. This mosaic is skillfully done, using foreshortening and perspective. It contains only four colors: red, brown, black, and white.

The key pattern
This is a well-known pattern that decorates many Greek paintings and vases. It is called the Greek key pattern because *key* means "meander" in Greek. A meander is a continuous rectangular pattern that keeps turning in on itself.

Glittering walls
Floor mosaics had to be smooth and flat, but wall mosaics could be more uneven. Light reflected off the shiny surfaces, making the picture glitter.

THE DEVELOPMENT OF SCULPTURE

Sculptors made statues to decorate temples, tombs, monuments, and homes. They used a number of techniques and various materials. Although most originals have been lost, many Roman copies of Greek statues have survived.

Classical sculpture

By Classical times, sculptors could show the body in a relaxed-looking, lifelike way. Legs placed apart showed movement, while faces looked gentle and smiling. Flowing clothes were gracefully folded, or bodies were naked with every muscle showing.

Themis, the Goddess of Justice, from Ramnous Attica in Greece, c. 3rd century BC, 6 feet, 7 inches (2 m), marble

Themis is the Greek goddess of justice. In Greek mythology, Themis was the daughter of Uranus and Gaia and the second wife of Zeus. Historically a goddess of order and assemblies, the word *themis* has now come to mean "law" in Greek.

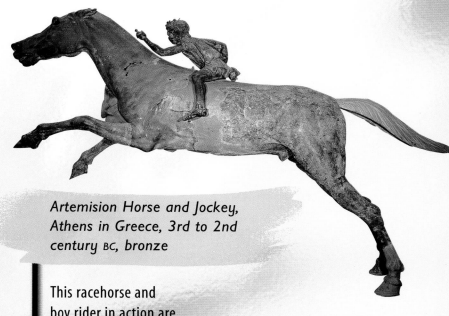

Stone statues

Large blocks of stone were difficult to move, so rough shapes of statues were cut in the quarry. Artists later carved details in workshops. Artists painted statues with bright colors, most of which have been worn away. They sometimes used glass or colored stones for eyes.

Expression and proportion

As sculptors of the Classical period became more skilled, they began producing portraits of real people. Even so, it was important to give them perfect-looking bodies.

Later, during the Hellenistic period, artists became interested in truthful images. They were not afraid to show people's old age or deformities.

Artemision Horse and Jockey, Athens in Greece, 3rd to 2nd century BC, bronze

This racehorse and boy rider in action are so realistic that they look as if they are about to gallop away! This is not a real portrait but was made to show how jockeys rode bareback and were usually servants, while racehorses were noble, expensive animals. Hellenistic sculptors made their work as lifelike as possible. Notice the boy's tousled hair.

Lost-wax sculptures

In the lost-wax process, artists made a clay core and stuck pins in it. Then, they molded wax around it to make the shape of the statue. They coated this with more clay, leaving a hole in the bottom. They heated it so the wax melted and ran out, leaving a space between the two amounts of clay. They then poured molten (melted) bronze into the hole. When it had set, they removed the clay, leaving the finished statue.

ART FOR THE GODS

Until the Hellenistic period, Greek artists often included gods and goddesses in their work. The Greeks believed in many gods and goddesses and had hundreds of stories about them. Gods and goddesses were said to control all aspects of life and death and to have the same emotions as humans. They could come to earth in a human shape, if they wished, and change people's lives.

Art and prayer

Greek temples, statues, and friezes were dedicated to the gods. Vase paintings show soldiers pouring wine into a bowl on the altar or onto the ground before leaving home. They are asking the gods for victory in battle. People prayed to statues of the gods and made sacrifices to them. Statues were brightly painted or made of precious materials. Many were huge, and by the Classical period they were incredibly lifelike.

Varvakeion Athena, *Athens in Greece, c. 400 BC, height 3 feet, 5 in. (1.05 m), marble*

Athena was the patron goddess of the city of Athens and also the goddess of wisdom and warfare. This marble statue was copied from a much larger one that stood in the Parthenon (see opposite). On Athena's helmet are flying horses and a sphinx (half human, half beast). The goddess's gently flowing hair and strong facial features were signs of Greek beauty.

The Parthenon Frieze, Phidias, c. 438 BC, 525 feet (160 m) in length, marble

This continuous frieze ran all around the Parthenon. The backgrounds were painted bright blue and red. Metal ornaments were added and the rest was painted in bright colors. It must have shone with color.

Friezes

A Greek sculptor named Phidias carved a frieze on the Parthenon. The frieze showed scenes from the Great Panathanaea festival. This was when the people of the city paid tribute to the goddess Athena.

No one knows who chose the subjects for the sculptures in Greek temples, but they show us what mattered to the people. Most temples had friezes, but the decoration of the Parthenon was by far the most ambitious ever attempted by the Greeks.

The Great Goddess Athena

A 39-feet (12-m) high statue of the goddess Athena originally stood in the Parthenon. Covered in gold, ivory, and colored stones, she was made by Phidias, who created powerful yet graceful sculptures. The statue of Athena must have looked startling to people entering the temple.

SCULPTURE FOR ALL

Not all sculpture was huge or made for public places. Some statuettes (mini statues) and small reliefs were made for people's homes. In addition to stone (marble, limestone, and **alabaster**) and metal (gold, silver, lead, bronze, and iron), sculptors used ivory, bone, amber, wax, wood, and especially terracotta.

Developing styles

Like the larger sculptures, these smaller sculptures show the same styles that developed through each period. Favorite subjects were human and animal figures. The sculptures were simply designed, but looked more relaxed and detailed by the Classical and Hellenistic periods. A lot of terracotta sculptures have been found in tombs. Many small sculptures were used as handles on vase lids.

This statuette is of two girls playing the popular Greek game of knucklebones. Even though it is small, the poses are graceful and lifelike.

Girls Playing, c. 340 BC, 5½ in. (14 cm), terracotta

Colors of clay

Terracotta statuettes, like stone and wood, were painted brightly. Archaic statuettes of gods and goddesses were usually painted black, white, red, and blue. Often these colorful creations had a more practical use as jugs or bottles.

Many later terracotta statuettes were little models of people doing everyday things such as kneading bread, taking care of children, cutting wood, or cutting hair. By Hellenistic times, these statuettes were extremely popular. They are simple but charming. If you have ever tried making a clay model, you will know how difficult such a statuette would be to make!

Painted wood or beeswax statuettes were also popular. The Greeks decorated their homes with little gods, goddesses, and heroes or symbols of family life (mainly women and children). Statuette-making was big business!

Everyday things

Sculptors also made objects that people used in the home, such as toys and cosmetic jars. Often these everyday things were buried with a person. Artists used as much artistic skill in these small household objects as they did for large statues. These terracotta feet from the 6th century BC are actually perfume bottles.

ANCIENT GREEK BUILDINGS

Buildings were designed to be as elegantly shaped as possible. Harmony and balance were most important to Greek architects. They created many splendid public buildings that have inspired architects throughout the ages. In fact, the idea of building as an art form came from the Greeks. Another Greek idea is that each building's measurements are the key to its beauty.

Building design

Temples and palaces of limestone or marble were magnificent, but normal houses were built with sun-dried mud bricks. Roofs were tiled. The rooms were built around an open courtyard, with windows facing inward.

By about 400 BC, open-air theaters were built. Seats made of stone were cut into a hillside, forming a kind of semicircle. The stage was low down in the center.

The most important Greek buildings were temples. The first temples (built as homes for the gods) were built with wood. Their flat roofs were first supported on tree trunk pillars (posts), then on rough columns of stone. From the 7th century BC, all public buildings, including temples, were made of limestone or marble.

Greek theater, Epidaurus, c. 450 BC, stone

Greek theaters were brilliant examples of engineering and art. Cut into hillsides, they were designed so that everyone could see and hear everything that happened on stage.

Erechtheion, Acropolis in Athens, 421–409 BC, marble

The Erechtheion is an Ionic (see below) temple built near the Parthenon in Athens. It is famous for its fine proportions. Here, six statues of women took the place of columns, their hats holding up the capitals. Human-shaped columns are called caryatids.

Architectural styles

There were two main architectural styles in Greek temple building: the Doric and the Ionic. The Doric was popular in mainland Greece. Columns and capitals (the tops of columns) were plain. In eastern parts of Greece and the islands, the Ionic style was more common. Columns were thinner and capitals were decorated with "volutes" (swirls carved into the top four corners).

Another style, Corinthian, had carvings in the shape of acanthus (a prickly plant) leaves on the capitals. The Greeks did not use the Corinthian style much, but the Romans loved it.

RELIGIOUS BUILDINGS

Religious buildings, such as shrines and temples, were often the target of enemy soldiers when the city states were at war. When the Persians invaded in 490 BC, they destroyed many temples. The biggest of these was the **Acropolis**, a temple to Athena, in Athens. When the Persians were driven out in 479 BC, the Athenians decided to rebuild the Acropolis. They also built an even more magnificent temple called the Parthenon.

Home for a goddess

The architect Ictinus designed and built the Parthenon between 447–438 BC. This was the Classical period. The Parthenon was designed with such a sense of balance and harmony that it is still considered to be one of the greatest buildings ever constructed.

Greek temples were open structures. The Parthenon rose up above Athens as a gleaming, white-columned monument. Measurements were figured out mathematically, giving the temple perfect proportions.

The Parthenon, c. 447–438 BC, 230 x 98 feet (70 x 30 m), marble

Beautiful buildings

Beauty and religion were important to the Greeks. By the Classical period, architects who designed religious buildings or monuments were valued highly.

Greek artists learned that our eyes can play tricks—straight lines do not always look straight. Using optical illusions, they could make buildings look striking and well balanced.

Temple of Athena Nike, c. 425 BC, marble

Nike was the goddess of victory. This miniature Ionic style temple was built in the Acropolis after the Parthenon was completed.

How the Parthenon was built

The foundations of the Parthenon were made from limestone, but the main building was marble. Architects gave the stonemasons (stonecutters and carvers) instructions for precise block sizes and shapes, which they cut using chisels and mallets. Finished blocks of stone were eased into place using ropes, pulleys, and levers. Pieces of metal called cramps held them in place.

The columns were made to lean slightly inward, drawing the eye upward. The base of the temple curved at the center to stop it from looking as though it were sagging. Phidias, the sculptor, designed the relief carvings and the statues inside, but most were made by skilled craftsmen. The statue of Athena (page 20) was heavily decorated with gold. It cost more than the Parthenon itself.

THE SEARCH FOR BEAUTY

The Greeks' fascination with the mind and beauty brought the most talented among them together. They discussed and criticized paintings, statues, and buildings, inspiring artists to create even greater works.

Artists searched for beauty, harmony, and a better understanding of people and the powers that control us. When they began experimenting, they introduced many new ideas about art to the world. Some of these ideas have lasted for centuries.

Woman Spinning, c. 500 BC, black and red paint on white-ground jug

Aritsts coated some vases with white paint and later added outline drawings in black and red paint. Women were often pictured on these vases in graceful poses, often at their daily tasks. On this jug, a woman is spinning. In her left hand she holds a distaff, which was a stick of wood or metal with a spike at one end and a handle at the other. It holds a ball of wool or flax. In her right hand, she spins the wool or flax into thread. This simple picture uses only the lines and colors necessary to give all this information in a balanced and clear way.

Greek inspirations

The ancient Greeks have influenced artists throughout history. The Romans were fascinated by them and copied much of their art, including their ideas, beliefs, and writings, especially poems, plays, and stories.

Nearly 1,000 years later, the Italians began to study the Greeks once more. This became a rebirth of thought and art and was later called the **Renaissance**.

Even today, throughout the world, many buildings resemble grand Classical temples. Paintings and statues are modeled on the Greeks' perfect proportions and balance. Pottery designs are inspired by their vases. The ancient Greeks gave us the idea that art means beauty. Artists have been affected by this idea ever since.

Greek Woman, c. 370 BC, marble

Although she seems a bit stiff, see how lifelike this statue's hands look and how her clothes gently drape and fold. Soon, Greek sculptors produced even more lifelike work in relaxed and natural poses.

Useful evidence

The fact that Greek artists liked to show things as lifelike and realistic helps us to find out about the ancient Greeks. Studying their art shows us how important music and sports were to them. We can find out about their battles, armor, and tactics. We can also discover details about their daily life. We know the types of thing that happened at their parties. We know how they did their laundry. We know how they taught their children.

TIMELINE

FIND OUT MORE

You can find out more about ancient Greek art in books and on the Internet. Use a search engine such as www.yahooligans.com to search for information. A search for the words "Greek art" will bring back lots of results, but it may be difficult to find the information you want. Try refining your search to look for some of the ideas mentioned in this book, such as "frescoes."

Books

Hatt, Christine. *Ancient Greece*. Chicago, Heinemann Library, 2005

Langley, Andrew. *Ancient Greece*. Chicago, Raintree, 2005

GLOSSARY

Acropolis fortress on a hill where Greek citizens could go for safety

alabaster translucent (semi see-through), creamy-white stone

apprentice person learning a trade or craft by working with a skilled worker

Archaic period (700–500 BC) when artists had to follow set rules when depicting objects and people

architect the word means "master builder" in ancient Greek. Architects design and construct buildings.

black-figure style using red clay backgrounds, artists painted black pictures and patterns

bronze long-lasting brownish gold metal. It is a mixture of copper and tin.

Classical period (500–323 BC) when artists showed a better understanding of proportion, weight, and movement, and art became more natural looking

encaustic method of painting using burned wax

fresco painting made on damp, freshly plastered walls

frieze band or strip of decoration used to decorate a wall or piece of pottery

Geometric period (1100–700 BC) when using lines and simple shapes was popular

Hellenistic period (323–100 BC) when artists developed even more skills in showing natural forms and also included flowing and magnificent details

limestone creamy-white rock used for building and carving

marble hard rock that comes in many colors. It can be polished to a high shine.

mural painting made directly on the wall of a building. A fresco is a type of mural.

optical illusion appearance of things that tell your eyes something is there that is not really there at all

parchment animal skin that is scraped, dried, and treated as a writing surface

Parthenon largest temple in the Acropolis at Athens

pigment colored powder made from plants, minerals, or animals and mixed with various liquids to make paint

proportion measurements of different parts and how they look together

red-figure style from about 510 BC, artists painted the background of their pottery black, leaving the figures unpainted so they appeared red

relief raised carved picture

Renaissance time of experiment in Europe when the skills of ancient Greece and Rome were studied and admired

symmetry same on both sides

tempera paint in which the pigment (color) is mixed with egg

terracotta means "baked earth." It is a clay, usually brownish-red, used to make pottery, tiles, and statues.

INDEX

Numbers in plain type (24)
refer to the text.

Numbers in bold type (**28**)
refer to an illustration.